Series editor: Lesley Sims

Designed by
Katarina Dragoslavić

Based on original material by
Caroline Young and John C. Miles
Original consultant: John Robinson

First published in 2004 by Usborne Publishing Ltd.,
Usborne House, 83-85 Saffron Hill, London EC1N 8RT, England.
www.usborne.com
Copyright © 2004, 1988 Usborne Publishing Ltd.

There are lots more great stories for you to read:

Usborne Young Reading: Series One
Aladdin and his Magical Lamp
Ali Baba and the Forty Thieves
Animal Legends
Stories of Dragons
Stories of Giants
Stories of Gnomes & Goblins
Stories of Magical Animals
Stories of Pirates
Stories of Princes & Princesses
Stories of Witches
The Burglar's Breakfast
The Dinosaurs Next Door
The Monster Gang
Wizards

Usborne Young Reading: Series Two
Aesop's Fables
Gulliver's Travels
Jason & The Golden Fleece
Robinson Crusoe
The Adventures of King Arthur
The Amazing Adventures of Hercules
The Amazing Adventures of Ulysses
The Clumsy Crocodile
The Fairground Ghost
The Incredible Present
The Story of Flying
The Story of Trains
Treasure Island

The Story of
Ships

Jane Bingham

Illustrated by
Colin King

Reading Consultant: Alison Kelly
University of Surrey Roehampton

Contents

Chapter 1
Crossing the water   3

Chapter 2
Ships of the Ancient World   12

Chapter 3
Raiders, traders and explorers   19

Chapter 4
Great adventures   29

Chapter 5
Pirates and wars   38

Chapter 6
The last days of sails   46

Chapter 7
All kinds of ships   56

Chapter 1

Crossing the water

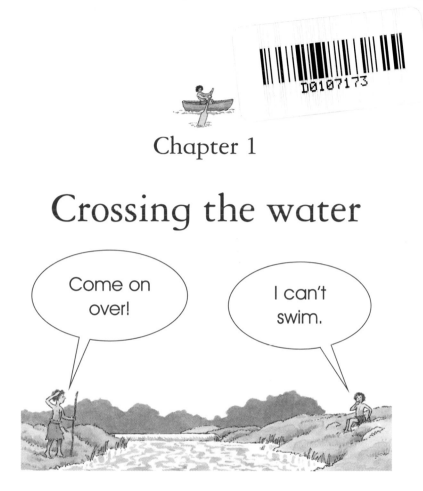

Thousands of years ago, there were no ships or boats. If you were born on one side of a river, that's where you stayed. But people dreamed of crossing rivers and seas.

People had noticed logs that floated on water. But they didn't do anything with them until a brave man tried to balance on one.

To his delight, he could paddle across the river. Steering the log wasn't easy... but falling off was.

Some people tied logs together to make a raft. Rafts could carry goods as well as people, but they were very hard to move along.

One day, someone had a fantastic idea. "Why don't we cut a log in half and hollow it out?" he said to his tribe. They thought he was crazy but they helped anyway.

The men used animal horns to hollow out the wood. To make the work easier, they lit a fire in the log to burn out the middle.

It was the world's first boat.

In some parts of the world,
people began to make
boats from animal
skins. First, they
sewed the
skins
together.

Then they
made a frame
from thin pieces
of wood.

Finally, they stretched the skins
over the frame and covered them
with tar to keep the water out.

At first, people pushed boats along with their hands. It was hard work. They soon realized what they needed was some sort of paddle.

Wooden paddles pushed boats along faster and helped people to steer.

After paddles came oars. These were much better because they were held in place by loops on each side of the boat.

But rowing was exhausting, so the rowers still didn't get very far...

until a bright rower realized he could use the wind to help.

Soon, everyone was making sails from animal skins and leaves. Some sails worked better than others.

The first great sailors lived on small islands in the South Pacific and sailed between the islands in wooden canoes.

Some brave islanders sailed for hundreds of miles. They found their way by watching the position of the sun and stars.

They also knew that birds flew between islands and clouds hovered over land, so they could tell if an island was nearby.

11

Chapter 2

Ships of the Ancient World

The Ancient Egyptians lived by the River Nile. They needed boats for fishing and taking food to market. To begin with, they made boats from reeds that grew by the Nile.

They tied the dried reeds into
bundles and made the bundles into
a boat. The only problem was the
reeds were not very strong.

So, they started building stronger, longer boats out of wood. These were strong enough to carry the massive stones used to build their pyramids and temples.

The Egyptians also used their boats to trade goods all over the Mediterranean.

It took up to thirty men to sail a trading boat. Some rowed and some looked after the sails. Two other sailors guided the boat with large steering oars.

Hey, you up there ripping the sail! Stop acting like a fool!

The Ancient Greeks built long, narrow galley ships. They used these for trading and fighting, though not at the same time. Galleys had both sails and oars, but sailors took down the sails before a battle.

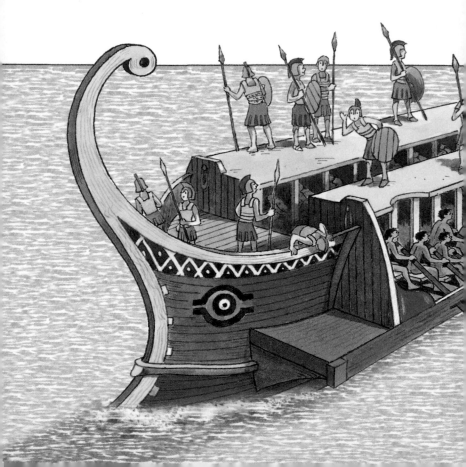

Galleys were rowed by slaves
who sat on benches inside the ship,
in rows of two or three.

The Romans built large trading and fighting ships too. Roman traders sailed far and wide in search of exotic goods. They brought back silk and spices from Asia, and elephants from Africa.

Did I mention I don't like heights?

Chapter 3

Raiders, traders and explorers

Around a thousand years ago, fierce Viking raiders began to attack parts of Europe. They sailed from Scandinavia in long ships – or longships – that sped through the waves.

19

But the Vikings were explorers too, taking voyages to unknown lands. When they arrived at a new place, some Vikings stayed. Many settled in Greenland and some even reached North America.

20

While the Vikings were exploring, so were sailors from China. They set off in junks, which could travel long distances thanks to their large sails.

There are records of Chinese traders and explorers visiting India and Africa. Some may even have reached Australia.

Chinese sailors were often a long way from land – too far to use clouds or birds to see where they were. To find their way over the seas, they invented the compass. This had a magnetic needle that pointed north.

They also invented the rudder, a piece of wood fixed to the stern, or

back, of a boat. It could move in the water, which made steering much easier.

Meanwhile, people in Europe were building strong sailing ships they named cogs. Like the Romans a thousand years before, they used their cogs for carrying goods and to fight each other.

Cogs were fitted with fighting platforms at the front and back of the ship. At first, sailors took them down after each battle. Soon, they simply left them up.

Sailors weren't just worried about enemy ships. They also feared attack from sea monsters and made up terrible stories about them, although they didn't really exist.

Monster ahead!

Cogs had a crow's nest on the
mast, where the look-outs stood.
This was very high up,
but it gave a good
view of what
was coming next.

Merchants went on long voyages to sell their goods, but life on board was no fun.

They had to sleep squashed together...

Let me just measure your space.

...and they were stuck with dry or salted food, because fresh food quickly rotted. Many grew sick.

When they weren't sick, they were bored. During the long months at sea, there was very little for passengers to do. They played the same games, over and over again, just to pass the time.

Sailors, on the other hand, didn't have a moment's peace. Sailing was hard and dangerous. Men often fell overboard and they weren't always rescued. But the worst job of all was being a galley slave.

Slaves sat inside the stuffy, smelly merchant ship, with rats crawling over their toes. Whenever the wind dropped, they rowed... and rowed... sometimes for days on end.

Chapter 4

Great adventures

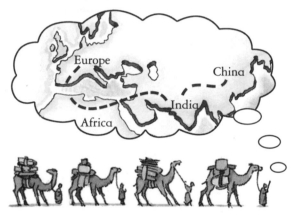

Merchants bringing goods from the East journeyed over land to the coast of North Africa, where they sailed to Europe. But explorers were convinced there was a quicker way from the East by sea.

In 1488, Bartholomew Diaz set off from Portugal and sailed around the tip of Africa.

He got halfway to India, but he didn't realize it was there. So, he turned back before he reached his goal.

Ten years later, the explorer Vasco da Gama also sailed south from Portugal.

Like Diaz, Vasco da Gama sailed around Africa. Unlike Diaz, he kept going until he reached land.

Da Gama had discovered a new route to the East.

The sea captain Christopher Columbus had a different plan. While many people thought the world was flat, he was sure it was round. So, he decided to sail west instead.

He planned to sail around the world until he reached China and India.

In 1492, Columbus left Spain with three ships. He sailed for over two months, but he didn't find the East.

After nine weeks at sea, the look-out shouted, "Land ahoy!" Columbus jumped up and down with excitement.

"We've sailed all the way to China!" he cried. In fact...

...they had reached North America. But Columbus had no idea. He was so sure he had found China, he sailed on in search of Japan...

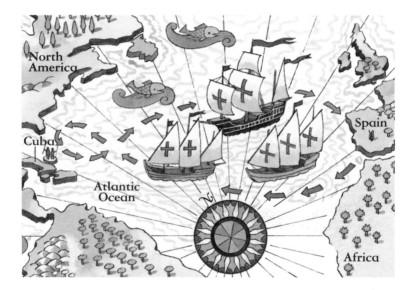

...and reached Cuba. Then he cheerfully sailed back to Spain, and told the king and queen he had found a new way to China.

Columbus went back to America
several times but he never knew he
had discovered a new continent.

35

Before long, every ruler in Europe wanted to find new land. In 1577, the English queen, Elizabeth, sent Francis Drake to South America.

"Attack the Spanish ships and take their treasure," she ordered, "and look for new land."

I want a country named after me!

Lizland? I like it!

Drake set sail from England in his small ship, the *Golden Hind*.

Over the next three years, he sailed all the way around the world.

It's good to be home!

Wait till they see all the gold we've brought!

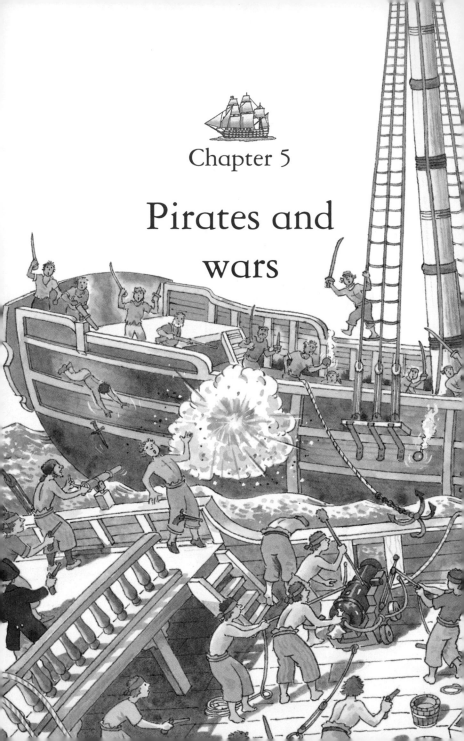

Chapter 5

Pirates and wars

Soon, thousands of ships were
sailing with precious cargoes.
They were easy targets for pirates.

Pirates would attack and steal the treasure. If they liked the look of a ship, they stole that too.

Blackbeard, one of the scariest pirates at sea, stuck burning ropes in his beard as he attacked.

There were even female pirates, such as Mary Read and Ann Bonney, who were fierce fighters.

Pirate ships were small and good for quick raids. But bigger ships were needed to fight major sea battles.

So, some countries began to build ships they named "men-of-war". The largest had over a hundred guns and nine hundred men. The only problem was finding enough men to sail them...

You'll do! Come with me.

Few people wanted to sail, and no wonder. From dawn to dusk they were hard at work.

I must have scrubbed this deck 1,000 times.

Ow! I think that burst my eardrum.

BANG!

Any sailor who refused
to work was beaten.

To make things worse, the food
was disgusting. For months, sailors
lived on stale, dry biscuits, salty
meat and hard maggoty cheese.

With no fresh fruit or vegetables,
many sailors died.

But there were more important things to worry about than bad food. While early warships had used cannons, newer ones were built that fired shells.

BOOM!

POW!

Wooden ships stood no chance against the new guns. Shipbuilders quickly came up with the answer, protecting their ships with iron plates. The first of these were used in the American Civil War.

Soon, battleships became even stronger.

The Devastation, built in 1872, had guns set in turrets. They could be turned to fire in any direction.

In 1906, the Dreadnought was launched. It had five gun turrets and was completely covered in steel.

Chapter 6

The last days of sails

It wasn't only warships that were changing. Around 1710, the first steam engine had been invented – and ships powered by steam didn't need the wind or oars.

Early steamships had two paddle wheels on the outside, driven by a steam engine. They still had sails though, just in case the engine broke down.

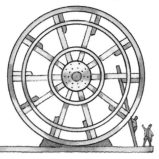

In the 1840s, a new kind of steamship was designed, with a propeller at the back. The propeller was turned by a single wheel inside the body of the ship.

Most people thought propellers worked better than paddles, but they couldn't prove it. So, two captains decided to test them both. They held a tug-of-war between two ships of about the same size.

First, the ships were joined by a strong cable. Then they steamed in opposite directions. The propeller ship won easily.

Although steam engines were very powerful, they didn't replace sails at first. Sailing ships were still used for long voyages.

In the 1800s, millions of people sailed from their homes in Europe to find a better life in a new country. They left for America, Australia and New Zealand.

Rich passengers had a very comfortable journey. They ate good food and relaxed in lounges.

Poorer passengers had a miserable time. There was so little space, they were all squashed in together.

They had to bring their own food and cook it themselves. And when the weather was bad, they were locked below deck.

The fastest sailing ships of all —
faster even than steamships — were
clippers. They sped across the
oceans, carrying goods that had
to be delivered quickly.

In 1848, when gold was found in
California, clipper captains raced
each other to reach it first. And, in
1866, the clippers *Ariel* and *Taeping*
raced from China to London. After
ninety-nine days at sea, the *Taeping*
won — by just half an hour.

The problem was that clippers needed strong winds to sail. They could speed along out at sea, but then the Suez Canal was opened, giving a shortcut to China.

Steamships sailed through it easily, but there wasn't enough wind for clippers. Soon, no one was using clippers any more.

Passenger sailing ships were not wanted either. Instead, steamship companies built ocean liners. These were vast floating hotels, with hundreds of bedrooms, shops, restaurants and ballrooms. Some even had a post office.

Oops!

Before a liner set off on a voyage, its crew had to carry masses of supplies on board.

Chapter 7

All kinds of ships

Some ship builders were more
interested in underwater boats.
They wanted to build submarines –
ships that could travel underwater
and launch surprise attacks on
other ships.

The first real submarine was built in 1798. To float on the surface it had a sail.

But when the submarine dived underwater, its sail folded away and it used a propeller to move.

Today, mini-subs are used to repair cables on the seabed...

...and *bathyscaphes* explore the deepest oceans.

Ships go much faster when they're not pushing through water, so inventors worked on ships to travel above the water. They came up with hovercrafts. These skim over the sea's surface, held up by a cushion of air.

Keep it steady!

Hovercrafts are especially useful for moving through swamps.

Help!

Hydrofoils, which speed through the water on undersea wings, are also quicker than ordinary ships.

Modern cargo ships don't go as fast as clippers but they hold much more. Biggest of all are oil tankers.

Oil tankers are too large to fit in a port. So, they pump oil into tanks in the sea. Some tankers are so vast the crews get around on bikes.

But boats today aren't only used for carrying goods and people. Many are sailed for fun.

And, just like the clipper captains of two hundred years ago, sailors love a race.